Original title:
Vivid Pales Along the Dragon Wing

Author: Kene Elistrand
ISBN HARDBACK: 978-1-80562-458-5
ISBN PAPERBACK: 978-1-80563-979-4

The Whirling Whispers of Skies

The clouds begin to dance and sway,
A symphony of whispers at play.
Gentle breezes weave their tales,
In the twilight where magic prevails.

Stars peek from their velvet shroud,
As shadows gather in a proud crowd.
Moonlight spills like silver thread,
A blanket for dreams just ahead.

Echoes of laughter drift on high,
Carried on wings of an evening sigh.
Mysteries twinkle, secrets to share,
In the vast expanse of the midnight air.

The ancient trees sway with grace,
Guardians of dreams in this sacred space.
Roots like fingers clutching the earth,
Nurturing whispers of life and rebirth.

In the hush of the world, hear the call,
Of whispers that rise and softly fall.
For in every gust, a story told,
In the whirling skies, brave and bold.

The Tints of a Dreamt Cosmos

In the cradle of night, colors blend,
A canvas where tales and visions send.
Palettes of stars, in splendor ignite,
Painting worlds in the hush of twilight.

Whispers of dreams float on the breeze,
Hues of wonder hidden in trees.
Crimson, azure, and emerald gleam,
Each tint reflecting a long-lost dream.

Galaxies twirl in a cosmic waltz,
Inviting the heart to see past the faults.
With every glance, new shapes arise,
Awakening marvels in starlit skies.

The tapestry stretches beyond the night's reach,
With lessons and wonders only they teach.
In the quiet, there's magic untold,
In the tints of a cosmos, both vivid and bold.

So look to the heavens with eyes wide and bright,
Let your spirit dance in the shimmering light.
For every hue holds a story to claim,
In the dreamt cosmos, where we're all the same.

Resonance of Light Upon Wings of Fire

In twilight's glow, the embers dance,
Whispers of courage, a fleeting chance.
The phoenix rises, flames alight,
Illuminating shadows, chasing the night.

With every beat, the heart ignites,
Boundless sky, where hope unites.
In dreams we soar on wings unstained,
Resonance of light, forever unchained.

Through storms we fly, with courage bold,
A story of valor, waiting to be told.
Every spark a promise, every flame a chance,
To dance with the cosmos in a golden trance.

Chasing the Glint of Chimerical Heights

Upon the dawn, a shimmer calls,
Whispers of magic behind the walls.
With every step, the spirit climbs,
Chasing the glint of celestial rhymes.

Through forests deep and rivers wide,
The heart beats faster, dreams collide.
Wings of wonder, through clouds they sweep,
In search of treasures, promises to keep.

Golden horizons, where shadows fade,
Chimerical heights, where hopes are laid.
In the realm of visions, we freely roam,
Crafting our legends, forging a home.

Spectrum's Embrace in a Mythical Flight

In colors rich, the world unfolds,
Mystical tales in whispers told.
Underneath the rainbow's arch,
A journey begins, where dreams embark.

With every hue, the heart extends,
A dance of shades where magic bends.
In flight we weave, through skies so wide,
Chasing the spectrum where visions reside.

Oh, mythical night, your beauty rare,
In wings we trust, in starlight we dare.
Embrace the journey, the dreams we write,
In the magic of colors, we take our flight.

The Dusk's Brushstrokes on Ancient Wings

As dusk draws near with a tender sigh,
The canvas glows, where dreams fly high.
Ancient wings of wisdom soar,
Carving stories, legends of yore.

With brushstrokes soft, the sky ignites,
Echoes of time in gentle lights.
In whispers of night, the memories cling,
A dance of shadows, where echoes sing.

Through twilight's kiss, we find our way,
Guided by spirits that never sway.
In the heart of dreams, where wonders gain,
The dusk's embrace sings sweet refrains.

The Spectrum Beneath the Wings

Beneath the sky, where shadows play,
The wings unfold, in bright array.
A dance of hues, from dusk till dawn,
The world ignites, in colors drawn.

Whispers weave through azure skies,
As dreams take flight, where magic lies.
Each flutter bright, a tale untold,
In every shimmer, a heart of gold.

The gentle breeze, a soft caress,
Embracing all, with tenderness.
In twilight's song, the secrets call,
To those who dare, to rise and fall.

A canvas spun from wild delight,
With every breath, the chase ignites.
For beneath those wings, the spectrum glows,
In every heart, where wonder grows.

So let us soar through skies so vast,
While vibrant memories are cast.
In dreams we seek, where colors play,
The spectrum glows, come what may.

Dreamscapes in Mystic Colors

In dreamscapes deep, where whispers flow,
The colors blend, a radiant show.
With shadows dancing on the tide,
Awakening worlds where dreams abide.

Velvet nights and silver beams,
Awash with light, the starlit dreams.
A tapestry of hopes unfurled,
In mystic hues, a magic swirled.

With every step, a brush we hold,
To paint the nights with stories bold.
In florid shades of twilight's grace,
We chase the dawn, a sweet embrace.

Through misty paths, where secrets bide,
The colors shift, and stars collide.
Each vibrant hue, a spell we cast,
In dreamscapes rich, where shadows pass.

So come, dear hearts, and take my hand,
Together paint this wondrous land.
With every stroke, let spirits rise,
In mystic colors, 'neath the skies.

Chasing the Aurora's Embrace

In frosty air, the night ignites,
With colors swirling, pure delights.
The aurora dances, bold and bright,
A cosmic show, a heart's delight.

Each shimmer, like a lover's gaze,
Draws us near in a mystical haze.
We chase the light, through winter's chill,
Where magic whispers, time stands still.

Beneath the stars, the heavens sing,
As nature's brush gifts every wing.
In hues of green and blazing red,
The aurora's arms, where dreams are led.

With courage found in icy breaths,
We craft our tales beyond the depths.
In every loop, a wish we send,
To grasp the light, as hearts extend.

So let the night unfold its charms,
As we are wrapped in beauty's arms.
In chasing her, we come to see,
The aurora's embrace, wild and free.

Paintbrush of the Enchanted Gale

The winds do whisper tales of old,
With paintbrush bold, they weave and fold.
Each gust a stroke, of wonder true,
Enchanting hearts, with shades anew.

In emerald fields where blossoms sway,
The gale spins dreams along the way.
Through every twist, a story's spun,
In vibrant hues, where life is fun.

With every breath, the colors blend,
At twilight's call, where visions send.
The paintbrush dances, light as air,
Creating worlds, beyond compare.

In echoes soft, the laughter flows,
As petals drift where magic glows.
With every breeze that sweeps the land,
The heart's own canvas, rich and grand.

So let us join in nature's spell,
With joyous hearts, we weave so well.
For in this gale, our spirits soar,
The paintbrush strokes forevermore.

Starlit Strides of Hidden Wonders

In twilight's whisper, secrets loom,
Where shadows dance in soft perfume.
The path unfolds beneath the sky,
With starlit guides, we wander high.

Each step reveals a story's thread,
Of ancient dreams and words unsaid.
Beneath the moon's embracing glow,
We find the wonders life might show.

Through forests deep and rivers wide,
With every heartbeat, worlds collide.
The hidden tales enchant our minds,
As nature's magic intertwines.

So take my hand, let us explore,
These hidden wonders, evermore.
With every glance, a spark ignites,
In starlit strides, we chase the nights.

A tapestry of dreams unfurl,
Adventures wait with every twirl.
With courage found in moonlit hues,
We'll seek the paths we dare to choose.

The Color Wheel of Time's Wings

From morning's blush to evening's sigh,
Each hue a voice, a lullaby.
The color wheel spins round and round,
In every shade, a tale is found.

Golden rays and silver streams,
A dance of colors fuels our dreams.
With every stroke, a moment flies,
In time's embrace, the heart complies.

The vibrant reds of passion's call,
The calming blue that sings to all.
Each color speaks of love and loss,
A vivid canvas, our albatross.

Through swirling greens of whispered leaves,
To autumn's gold as daylight grieves,
Life paints us in its boldest style,
In every hue, a hopeful smile.

So let us bask in nature's art,
Embrace the colors of the heart.
For in their depths, we find our wings,
The color wheel of time's sweet things.

Ethereal Light and Winged Shadows

At dusk's embrace, the shadows play,
With wings of night that softly sway.
Ethereal light begins to glow,
As dreams awaken, rich and slow.

The whispers twirl on gentle air,
In silver beams, we shed our cares.
With every shadow, stories blend,
In twilight's arms, our spirits mend.

From starlit skies to whispered trees,
The world enchanted, bound to please.
With each soft flutter, secrets keep,
As light and shadow dance in sleep.

Oh, let us roam this magical land,
With every heartbeat, hand in hand.
The winged shadows guide our way,
Through realms of night to greet the day.

For in this balance, peace we find,
With ethereal light that fate has lined.
So let us walk where darings flow,
In realms where light and shadows grow.

The Ethereal Listeners in Color

Beneath the boughs where silence dwells,
The ethereal listeners weave their spells.
In vibrant hues, they catch our sighs,
As whispers float to endless skies.

With emerald thoughts and azure dreams,
They gather all our joyful streams.
Each brush of color paints a sound,
A symphony of souls unbound.

They listen close to hearts aflame,
Collecting wishes, learning names.
In amber tones of love laid bare,
Their colors weave a truth we share.

With gentle hands, they shape the air,
Transforming whispers into prayers.
In every shade, a tale revealed,
The ethereal listeners have healed.

So let us join this vibrant song,
With every shade, we all belong.
In colors bright, we'll find the way,
Together in this grand ballet.

Glimmers of a Forgotten Realm

In shadows deep, where whispers dwell,
A secret world, a mystic spell.
With trees that talk and rivers gleam,
Awake, the night, a gentle dream.

A silver moon, a guiding light,
Through emerald paths, the stars take flight.
Old tales of courage, lost and found,
In every breeze, a haunting sound.

Beneath the boughs, the fae do play,
In twilight's arms, they slip away.
With laughter soft, and hearts so bold,
They weave their magic, tales untold.

A glimmer bright, a portal wide,
Where time stands still and dreams abide.
To wander lost, yet feel so free,
In realms of light and memory.

So wander near, let spirit soar,
In glimmers rare, from days of yore.
For in that realm where wonders sing,
Eternal joy is found in spring.

Shades of Wind and Wonder

In gentle breeze, the whispers hide,
Secrets of worlds where dreams collide.
Through fields of gold, where daisies sway,
The winds of change will softly play.

With every gust, a story told,
Of fleeting hearts and spirits bold.
In shades of dusk, the colors bleed,
A tapestry of thought and deed.

So lift your gaze, let wonder flow,
Through earthly paths where shadows grow.
With every lilt, a song anew,
In shades of wind, your heart breaks through.

In skies of blue, the visions blend,
With laughter bright that knows no end.
As twilight falls, the stars appear,
A canvas wide that draws us near.

Embrace the night, let spirits twine,
In dreamy hues, the stars align.
For in this dance, we find our place,
In shades of wind, a warm embrace.

Dances of Color and Lore

In vibrant hues, the stories gleam,
Where every shade fulfills a dream.
The canvas wide, in motion flows,
With every brush, a tale bestows.

Through palettes rich, we weave our fate,
With laughter bright and hearts elate.
In dances bold, the colors play,
A symphony to seize the day.

In twilight's glow, the shadows blend,
Each brushstroke whispers, love transcends.
With laughter shared, the moments freeze,
In dances bright, our souls at ease.

Through cycles round, the seasons change,
In colors wild, we rearrange.
With every swirl, the past ignites,
In dances of endless, starry nights.

So let us paint the sky anew,
With every shade, a life imbue.
For in our hearts, the colors soar,
In dances bright, forevermore.

Colorful Reverberations in the Sky

Above the world, the colors burst,
With every hue, our spirits thirst.
In radiant arcs, the sunsets glow,
A canvas rich, a vibrant show.

The golden dawn, a promise bright,
With every day, a new delight.
In azure vast, the dreams take flight,
With swirling clouds, our hearts ignite.

Among the stars, the echoes play,
In shadows soft, where children lay.
With hopes aglow, they hum their tune,
Through colorful nights, beneath the moon.

In every spark, a story spins,
With laughter ringing, life begins.
From crimson dawn to twilight's shower,
We dance in time, with love as power.

So gaze above, let colors stream,
In every pulse, we join the dream.
For in the skies, our souls entwine,
In colorful waves, forever shine.

Whispers of Iridescent Feathers

In twilight's breath, the whispers sing,
A tapestry of colors, softly cling.
The feathers dance on gentle air,
Each stroke a dream laid bare.

They flutter near the silver brook,
Where secrets hide in every nook.
With every rustle, tales unfold,
Of ancient times and stories bold.

Beneath the stars, their flutters weave,
A melody that weaves reprieve.
In shadows cast by moonlit beams,
They sing of hope and whispered dreams.

The world stands still as night descends,
And in their twilight, the magic bends.
With iridescent sparkles bright,
They guide the heart through realms of light.

So listen closely, let them guide,
Each feather holds a tale inside.
For in the whispers, you will find,
The connection of the heart and mind.

Echoes of Celestial Scales

Beneath the vast, expansive sky,
The scales of stardust shimmer high.
With hues of cosmic, vibrant light,
They echo softly through the night.

Each scale a story, each gleam a song,
In the celestial dance, where we belong.
They ripple with the tides of fate,
A reminder that love can wait.

In galaxies where shadows creep,
The echoes of the heavens sweep.
They whisper secrets of the wise,
In shimmering patterns that arise.

With every twinkle, a promise made,
Of journeys taken, never strayed.
In cosmic tales, we find our place,
United in this vast embrace.

So gaze above at the endless seas,
For in the depths, the heart finds ease.
The echoes of the stars resound,
In every soul, their truth is found.

Dance of the Chromatic Shadows

In twilight's haze, shadows entwine,
A dance of colors, soft and fine.
They flicker lightly, a playful game,
In hues of joy, they spark the flame.

With every turn, the darkness sways,
In chromatic realms where magic plays.
They whisper secrets lost in time,
In rhythms soft, a gentle rhyme.

As dawn awakens the night's embrace,
Shadows weave, a celestial lace.
The colors blend, a vibrant show,
In every heart, they hum and glow.

So join the dance and feel the thrill,
In shades of twilight, dreams fulfill.
Let every shadow tell its tale,
In the cosmic waltz, we shall not pale.

For in this realm of shifting light,
Life's dance unfurls through day and night.
With every shadow, step we take,
A world alive, for hearts to wake.

Celestial Tints of the Serpent

Amidst the stars, the serpent glides,
In celestial tints where magic hides.
With scales that shimmer like the sun,
Each twist and turn is a journey begun.

Through cosmic rivers, serpents roam,
In colorful dreams, they find a home.
With a flick of their tongue, they taste the light,
A dance of colors, bold and bright.

They spiral through the voids of space,
Leaving trails of stardust lace.
In every curve, a story spun,
The serpent whispers, we are one.

So heed the call of the vibrant night,
For in their depths, we find our sight.
With celestial tints, they guide the way,
To brighter tomorrows, come what may.

Embrace the magic woven tight,
In scales of color, pure delight.
The serpentine dance, our hearts in flight,
Together, we shall soar, ignite.

The Wings of Time's Palette

In twilight's embrace, colors collide,
Where whispers of dreams in stillness abide.
Each brushstroke of memory, softly it glows,
Within the heart's canvas, the essence flows.

A fluttering moment, caught in a frame,
Time weaves its stories, never the same.
With hues of regret and joys intertwined,
The wings of the past in the canvas aligned.

As shadows and light play a delicate game,
Each color, a touch of the soul's hidden flame.
The journey unfurls with each beat of the heart,
A palette of memories, artfully part.

Moments awaken, in whispers they sing,
The laughter of ages, the tales they bring.
In the gallery of life, we find our own way,
With the wings of time painting night and day.

So gather the hues, let your spirit take flight,
For the canvas of life is a wondrous delight.
Each moment preserved in the light of the mind,
With wings of time's palette, all beauty we find.

A Chorus of Dancing Shadows

In the moonlit hour, shadows take flight,
They dance on the edge of the flickering light.
A whispering breeze tells stories untold,
In the chorus of darkness, the magic unfold.

Figures entwined in a delicate sway,
Echoes of laughter that drift far away.
With each graceful step, the night starts to hum,
A symphony sung as the shadows succumb.

Between whispering pines and the stars up above,
The shadows are glimpses of stories we love.
Each flicker of movement, a tale intertwined,
In the depths of the night, hidden truths we find.

So join in the dance, let your spirit ignite,
For the shadows are echoes of dreams taking flight.
A chorus that's woven with threads of the night,
In the arms of the darkness, our hearts feel the light.

And as the dawn breaks, their presence will fade,
Yet the echoes of joy in our hearts will not shade.
For shadows may vanish, but memories stay,
A chorus of dancing, forever we play.

Dreamscapes of the Celestial Art

In the canvas of dreams, the stars paint the night,
With whispers of worlds that shimmer in light.
Each stroke of the cosmos, a tale of its own,
Where the heart finds its rhythm, and magic is sown.

Celestial wonders in beautiful hues,
A tapestry woven with delicate views.
In the depths of the sky, our fantasies soar,
Each dream an adventure, inviting us more.

Through cosmic meadows where starlight does weave,
The dreams gently beckon, inviting to believe.
A dance of existence, both fleeting and grand,
In the embrace of the night, where the cosmos will stand.

So drift in the visions, let your heart roam free,
Amongst the bright planets, where we long to be.
In the dreamscapes of night, let your spirit depart,
For the celestial art is a journey of heart.

With colors of starlight and shadows of grace,
Each moment a treasure, a beautiful space.
In the vastness of dreams, we find our own way,
In the dreamscapes of celestial art, we play.

The Symphony of Color and Wing

In gardens of wonder where colors unfold,
The symphony sings, both tender and bold.
With fluttering wings and blossoms in bloom,
Nature's sweet orchestra dispels all the gloom.

Each note of the breeze carries stories of old,
With whispers of petals, their fragrances told.
The dance of the butterflies, vivid and bright,
In the warmth of the sun and the coolness of night.

As raindrops like jewels kiss the earth with delight,
The harmony blossoms, a dazzling sight.
From meadows to mountains, a canvas of chance,
Where colors entwine in a jubilant dance.

Oh, join in the revelry, let spirits collide,
For the symphony beckons, let hearts open wide.
In the song of the colors, our souls intertwine,
With wings of pure joy, in the garden divine.

So gather the hues, let the music take flight,
In the symphony woven of day and of night.
For life is a canvas where colors engage,
In the symphony of color, let us turn the page.

The Dream Weaver's Palette

In a canvas spun of night,
Colors dance in soft delight,
Whispers echo through the air,
Dreams take shape with tender care.

Stars a-glimmer, tales untold,
Stories painted bright and bold,
Each brushstroke, a silent wish,
Melding realms where spirits swish.

Hues of hope and fear entwined,
In the silence, joy we find,
A tapestry of heart's embrace,
Weaved together, time and space.

Moonlight bathes the woven threads,
As every slumber gently spreads,
Crafting worlds with every sigh,
In the night, the dreams can fly.

With each dawn, the colors fade,
Yet in the heart, the dreams are laid,
A palette spun from love's own heart,
In dreams, we're never far apart.

Conversations with Celestial Beasts

In the hush of twilight's glow,
Beasts of legend softly show,
Eyes of wisdom, hearts of fire,
Speak of realms that lift us higher.

A dragon's scale reflects the stars,
Tales of time, of battles, scars,
With every word, the cosmos sways,
Echoing ancient, wondrous ways.

The phoenix sings of bright tomorrows,
In its song, the end of sorrows,
With each feather, hope takes wing,
In the heart, new life takes spring.

The unicorn prances, grace divine,
Hooves that dance on flickering line,
Sharing secrets of the night,
Whispering dreams, pure and bright.

In twilight's embrace, they depart,
Leaving imprints on the heart,
Conversations that foreverlast,
In their presence, shadows cast.

Ombre Echoes of Twilight

When the sun dips low in grace,
Shadows stretch to find their place,
Whispers twine in subtle tales,
As dusk unveils the evening sails.

Colors blend in shades of night,
Softly dimming, out of sight,
The horizon wears a cloak so fine,
Embraced by stars, they brightly shine.

Mists weave through the silent trees,
Carrying echoes on the breeze,
Each lilt a memory of light,
Turning day into velvet night.

In this twilight, dreams emerge,
Gentle hearts begin to surge,
With every star that takes its stand,
Ombre whispers beckon, hand in hand.

As shadows dance, the world does sigh,
In twilight's arms, we learn to fly,
Lost in realms where silence speaks,
Ombre echoes, the heart seeks.

The Radiant Wing's Lament

Beneath the weight of fleeting skies,
A radiant wing begins to cry,
Once it soared with endless grace,
Now it mourns a lost embrace.

Glistening feathers touch the ground,
Where once were dreams, now sorrow found,
Every breeze a memory stings,
As the heart of a bird it sings.

Twilight drapes the canopy fine,
A symphony of loss intertwines,
The world, a canvas soaked in tears,
Filled with whispers of ancient fears.

Yet in the night, a flicker glows,
Hope rises where the shadow grows,
The lament hums a soft refrain,
Of wings that yearn to fly again.

From the depths of pain and plight,
A new dawn breaks, a healing light,
The radiant wing, through trials bent,
Finds strength within its lament.

Murmurs of the Cosmic Canvas

Beneath the stars, the whispers play,
Across the night, where shadows sway.
Celestial tales in silence spun,
A tapestry of dreams begun.

Glimmers dance on the velvet dark,
Each twinkle holds a secret spark.
In cosmic winds, the stories drift,
A universe of endless gift.

Galaxies weave through time and space,
Starlit echoes leave their trace.
In every heart, the cosmos lies,
Waiting for the soul to rise.

Planets hum a lullaby sweet,
With every beat, our fates repeat.
In the silence, wisdom grows,
A breath of magic softly flows.

So close your eyes, embrace the night,
Become one with the glowing light.
For in the dark, the dreams will soar,
To cosmic shores forevermore.

Echoing Tales in Twilight Hues

In twilight's grasp, the whispers weave,
Old tales linger, hearts believe.
Beneath the arch of dusky skies,
Dreams unfurl like fireflies.

Each shadow holds a secret thread,
In the soft dusk, stories spread.
The moonlight bathes the world in grace,
Echoes dancing in time and space.

With every breeze, a song is born,
A symphony of night adorned.
In pools of light, the spirits speak,
Their ancient wisdom loud, yet meek.

The stars align in gentle sighs,
A canvas where the heart complies.
As darkness swirls, we lose our way,
Yet find the path where dreams can play.

So linger in the twilight glow,
Where echoed tales still gently flow.
For in this hour, both deep and true,
The world awakens, anew with hue.

A Dance of Shadows and Light

In the moon's embrace, shadows glide,
With light as partner, side by side.
A dance unfolds in perfect rhyme,
An evening waltz, a lift through time.

Whispers soft, as nightingale calls,
In the quiet glades, where magic falls.
Every flicker, a spark divine,
In harmony, their fates entwine.

Through rustling leaves, the stories bloom,
In twilight's breath, dispelling gloom.
Each shadow spins in radiant flight,
A ballet born of dark and light.

As spirits twirl in moonlit grace,
With every step, they find their place.
An echo of a forgotten dream,
In swirls of silver, they redeem.

So take my hand, we're set to roam,
Through realms of dusk, we make our home.
For in this dance, the heart takes flight,
Lost in the shadows, found in light.

Dreaming in Radiant Whispers

In realms where dreams begin to spark,
Whispers bleed in colors dark.
Each thought a thread, each breath a hue,
In vibrant strokes, the heart breaks through.

With eyes closed tight, the visions flow,
A garden blooms from seeds we sow.
In gentle night, our spirits fly,
Through unknown worlds, where wonders lie.

Conversations with the stars unfold,
In radiant tones, their tales retold.
Each droplet of night, a promise bright,
Guarding dreams 'til morning light.

Through silver beams, our voices blend,
In cosmic songs, on which we depend.
We weave our wishes, bold yet kind,
In radiant whispers, we are aligned.

So let us drift on stardust streams,
Awake in wonder, lost in dreams.
For in each heart, the universe sings,
A symphony of endless things.

Glimmers Between the Scales

In shadows where the secrets lie,
The scales reflect the moonlit sky.
Each glimmer tells a tale untold,
Of ancient bonds and hearts of gold.

Through emerald leaves the whispers weave,
A dance of light for those who believe.
Beneath the watchful, twinkling stars,
The magic lingers, near and far.

The scales, they shimmer with hope's embrace,
In twilight's breath, we find our place.
Each pulse, a memory softly spun,
In the heart of night, where journeys run.

With every flicker of soft light,
Dreams awaken, taking flight.
The forest sighs, a gentle song,
Where all the lost and found belong.

So listen close, let silence guide,
For in this realm, the worlds collide.
Each glimmer, a promise, bright and bold,
A tapestry of stories, waiting to unfold.

The Spectrum of Whispering Winds

A breeze flows softly through the vale,
Where whispers dance, and dreams unveil.
The colors blend, both bright and pale,
In nature's art, we find our trail.

Each gust a secret, gently shared,
Of hopes and wishes, truly dared.
The wind, a friend, both wild and free,
Carries the laughter of a tree.

Through valleys deep, on mountains high,
The winds converse, beneath the sky.
In every hue, a story spins,
A song of life, where love begins.

From amber leaves in autumn's glow,
To winter's chill and spring's soft show,
The spectrum paints a vibrant scene,
Of fleeting moments, lost and gleaned.

So let the winds their secrets tell,
In whispered tones where shadows dwell.
With open hearts, we chase the flow,
And in the winds, our spirits grow.

Chromatic Echoes in the Twilight Realm

In twilight's hush, colors collide,
Where echoes linger, deep and wide.
Each shade a memory, soft and clear,
A fleeting moment, always near.

The shadows stretch and twist in grace,
As dreams take form, without a trace.
In vibrant hues, the night unfolds,
With stories whispered, brave and bold.

Stars blink twice in a playful tease,
As magic ripples through the breeze.
In every flicker, a promise shines,
Of connection forged in celestial lines.

The twilight dances, wild and free,
Encasing souls in harmony.
In chromatic glows, we find our way,
A vivid journey, come what may.

So chase the echoes, seek the light,
In every heartbeat, take your flight.
For in the twilight's embrace we dwell,
In chromatic dreams, all is well.

Luminous Patterns of the Celestial Serpent

Through skies adorned with cosmic glow,
The serpent winds, both fast and slow.
Each scale a gem, a story spun,
In patterns bright, our lives begun.

With stars as eyes, it glides above,
A guardian spirit, full of love.
In luminous trails, it beckons near,
To secrets held, both far and dear.

In every twist, a chance to learn,
As galaxies in spirals turn.
The universe whispers in the dark,
In silver threads where dreams embark.

So dance with shadows, embrace the night,
For in the dark, we find our light.
In patterns woven, we are bound,
To the celestial, forever found.

Let go of fears, let spirits soar,
In luminous realms, we're evermore.
For in the serpent's graceful glide,
We find the magic, deep inside.

Kaleidoscope of the Mystic Sky

Beneath the heavens, colors blend,
Whispers of magic, light will send.
Stars are dancers, twirling bright,
Each flicker holds a tale of night.

Clouds like dreams in soft caress,
Creating patterns, none can guess.
The moon, a guardian, watches near,
Its silver glow, a beacon clear.

Colors shift in secret sway,
Painting skies with hues of play.
Mysteries born from twilight's grace,
In the dance, we find our place.

Winds carry whispers, soft and low,
Of hidden realms, we long to know.
The sky, a door to worlds untold,
A story of wonder, forever bold.

So gaze upon this mystic dome,
In its embrace, we find our home.
For every spark, a magic spark,
In the kaleidoscope, we embark.

Hues of Enchantment Rising

As dawn awakens, colors spill,
Chasing the shadows, calm and still.
Golden rays, a warm embrace,
Inviting dreams to find their place.

Petals bloom in vibrant hue,
Dewdrops glisten with morning's dew.
Nature, a canvas, fresh and bright,
Painting secrets in morning light.

Birdsongs whisper on the breeze,
Fluttering gently through the trees.
Each note a promise, pure and true,
Of magic hidden in every view.

The sky, a palette wide and vast,
Hues of enchantment, unsurpassed.
From rose to lavender's soft sigh,
In every glance, a piece of sky.

So let us wander through this morn,
With hearts wide open, dreams reborn.
In the tapestry of light we weave,
Endless wonders we believe.

The Glistening Tapestry Unfurls

Threads of silver, woven bright,
A tapestry of dreams takes flight.
Every shimmer, a story spun,
Beneath the gaze of the watching sun.

Each stitch carries whispers soft,
Of hopes and wishes, lost aloft.
In the fabric of night's sweet song,
We're where the endless tales belong.

Stars like jewels upon the seam,
Weaving magic into each dream.
Galaxies swirl in delicate trace,
A cosmic dance, a loving grace.

Patterns shifting, colors blend,
The universe, our truest friend.
In every fold, a secret gleams,
In the tapestry of our dreams.

So gather close, let stories dive,
In the glistening strands, we thrive.
For in this weaving, strange yet real,
Lies the enchantment that we feel.

Reflections of a Mythic Flight

On wings of wonder, spirits soar,
Through realms of lore, forever more.
Chasing shadows, dancing light,
In the heart of a mythic flight.

Beyond horizons, secrets beckon,
In whispered tales, the heart can reckon.
Clouds become castles in the air,
Each dream a thread, a silent prayer.

The winds recount the tales of old,
Of heroes brave, of hearts bold.
With every beat, the sky ignites,
In reflections of our soaring sights.

So let us glide on twilight's wings,
As stardust wraps around our strings.
In every leap, our spirits rise,
Into the realm where magic lies.

Together we'll weave through time and space,
In the tapestry of dreams we chase.
For in this journey, wild and bright,
We find ourselves in mythic flight.

The Palette of Starlit Halls

In chambers where the shadows play,
Colors whisper night and day.
Each hue a tale, each shade a dream,
In starlit halls, where wonders gleam.

The azure skies kiss golden light,
Guiding paths through velvet night.
Emerald glances tease the stars,
As magic mingles, soft and far.

Crimson echoes swirl and dance,
With every twirl, a fleeting chance.
Beneath the moon's soft silver gaze,
Lost in the art of night's embrace.

The palette swirls, a vibrant sea,
Drawing forth our destiny.
In every color, secrets bide,
In starlit halls, our fates collide.

So take my hand, let's drift and dive,
In realms where dreams are still alive.
Through the shadows, light will lead,
In these halls, we plant a seed.

Spiraling Hues of Ancient Legends

In whispers past, the legends call,
Spiraling hues that weave enthrall.
Each tale a brush, a vivid stroke,
In depth of night, the silence spoke.

Emerald flames dance with delight,
Unraveling the muted night.
With crimson threads of time unwound,
The essence of the lost is found.

A sapphire river flows through dreams,
Where ancient hearts burst at the seams.
The echoes travel through the air,
As we, the seekers, wander rare.

Each color tells of love and pain,
Of battles lost, of dreams we gain.
In spiraling hues, our spirits soar,
Awakening the tales of yore.

Through time's embrace, we linger still,
With whispered hopes, and trembling will.
A tale of ages, every hue,
In ancient legends, old yet new.

Echoes of Vibrant Sorrows

In echoes soft, the sorrows blend,
With vibrant hues that twist and bend.
Each tear a note in life's refrain,
A symphony of joy and pain.

Beneath the surface, colors cry,
In silent storms that never die.
A tapestry of loss and gain,
Weaved from the threads of dreams in vain.

The shadows speak in gentle tones,
Reminding us we're not alone.
A palette rich with shades of night,
Embracing darkness, seeking light.

Each sorrow's song, a vivid thread,
In every heart, the colors spread.
With every heartbeat, warmth will find,
The vibrant solace, intertwined.

So raise a glass to joys in sorrow,
And let the hues bring forth tomorrow.
In echoes sweet, our stories flow,
Uniting hearts, where sorrows glow.

Secrets beneath Shimmering Skies

Beneath the skies, where dreams reside,
Secrets linger, far and wide.
In whispers soft, they softly call,
From twilight's edge, they weave and sprawl.

The stars like lanterns gently glow,
With mysteries that time won't show.
In silver threads of night's embrace,
We search for truth in every space.

The moon's soft light unveils the past,
As shadows dance, and moments pass.
Each secret holds a deeper spark,
Guiding souls through velvet dark.

In shimmering skies, we find our way,
Where love and hope eternally stay.
Each secret woven into the night,
A tapestry of sheer delight.

So let us dream, let spirits rise,
Underneath these shimmering skies.
For every heart, a tale awaits,
In secrets shared, where magic resonates.

Chimeras in Celestial Hues

In shadows dance the dreams of night,
A tapestry of stars takes flight,
Chimeras weave in vibrant gaze,
Beneath the moon's enchanted blaze.

The colors swirl, a painter's hand,
On cosmic canvas, grand and grand,
With every stroke, new worlds awake,
In depths of skies, the heart will shake.

Mysteries twirl in twinkling sounds,
A symphony where magic bounds,
The whispers call from realms above,
As daybreak heralds night's soft love.

In silence held are secrets rare,
Each hue a tale spun through the air,
The chimeras soar, majestic, free,
In celestial hues, they beckon me.

So let the stars guide paths unknown,
Through cosmic realms, our spirits flown,
In colors bright, our dreams ignite,
Chimeras dance in endless night.

Canvas of Whirling Dreams

Upon a canvas vast and wide,
Where fantasies and hopes collide,
Brush strokes twirl in wild delight,
As day surrenders to the night.

The dreams take shape, and shadows play,
In vibrant hues of night and day,
Whirls of thoughts, like feathers glide,
On winds of magic, they shall ride.

In every corner, wonders bloom,
The whispers weave through quiet rooms,
A tapestry of deep desire,
Igniting hearts with sacred fire.

Each stroke a wish, each line a plea,
In this vast realm, we seek to see,
The colors swirl with secret grace,
In life's grand dance, we find our place.

So take this brush, and paint your dream,
Let visions flow like silver streams,
In a canvas where we break the seams,
And weave together whirling dreams.

Enigma of the Chromatic Winds

In whispers low, the breezes sing,
Of tales that time can't help but bring,
The chromatic winds, a lively dance,
Invite the hearts to take a chance.

They carry scents of worlds unseen,
Through valleys lush and forests green,
In every gust, a story told,
Of love and loss and dreams of gold.

As rainbows arch and colors blend,
The mysteries in stillness bend,
While every breath unveils a lore,
Of nature's pulse, forevermore.

The winds shall swirl, and spirits leap,
In cosmic rhythms, secrets keep,
A melody in every sigh,
Where wishes linger, soar, and fly.

So close your eyes, and tune your ear,
To every note the winds hold dear,
In spaces vast, where dreams begin,
Embrace the enigma of the winds.

Whirls of Cosmic Whisper

In depths of night, where silence hums,
The whispers soft like distant drums,
Across the stars, in gentle flow,
The cosmos spins, a tale to show.

With every breath, the galaxies sigh,
A secret dance 'neath velvet sky,
In twinkling lights, the stories weave,
Of hopes and dreams we dare believe.

Through swirling mists of time and space,
The echoes find their rightful place,
In bounds of magic, hearts unite,
As destiny ignites the night.

So let the whispers guide your way,
Through cosmic realms where spirits play,
In whirls of light, embrace the hue,
For in this dance, the world feels new.

With every twinkle, every gleam,
In cosmic whispers, find your dream,
Let stardust sprinkle on your soul,
As you become one with the whole.

Luminous Secrets of the Night

Whispers of stars in the velvet sky,
Guide us through shadows, where secrets lie.
Moonlight dances on leaves so bright,
Breathing magic into the heart of night.

Ancient trees cradle stories untold,
Their branches harbor the dreams of old.
Night blooms softly, with fragrance sweet,
In the silence, the world feels complete.

Wand of the wizard, a flicker of light,
Unlocks the door to the hidden sight.
Luminous paths where the wild things roam,
Inviting our spirits to find their home.

A breath of the night, a gentle sigh,
In twilight's embrace, we learn to fly.
With every blink, a new tale begins,
The luminous secrets where magic spins.

So let us wander through the night divine,
Where shadows whisper and stars align.
In the heart of darkness, we find our grace,
Embracing the wonders that time cannot chase.

Palette of the Behemoth

In the dawn's embrace, colors collide,
A canvas of giants, where dreams reside.
Brushstrokes of thunder in hues bold and free,
Painting the tale of the great mystery.

Mountains arise, draped in twilight's gown,
Their peaks piercing clouds, wearing crowns of brown.
The oceans below, a vast azure spread,
A palette of life where legends are bred.

Crimson sunsets ignite the vast sky,
With whispers of fire, the horizon sighs.
Majestic and timeless, the beasts roam wide,
Their colors a secret, their strength a guide.

Shadows and light dance in harmony,
Creating a world rich in symphony.
The behemoth's heart beats low and slow,
In each brushstroke, the stories that flow.

So treasure the canvas, embrace the sight,
In the palette of giants, find pure delight.
For every color tells tales untold,
Of a world that awaits, adventurous and bold.

Flight Over the Painted Horizon

Above the expanse, where dreams take flight,
Wings stretch wide in the canvas of light.
Clouds drift lazily, touched by the sun,
In a world where our journeys have just begun.

Painted horizons in shades of gold,
A tapestry woven with stories of old.
The whispers of winds beckon us near,
With each soft caress, we conquer our fear.

As the sun sets low, the sky ignites,
Crimson and violet fill the night's sights.
With every heartbeat, the heavens expand,
Inviting our souls to soar and to land.

The stars waltz gracefully, guiding the way,
Inviting the dreamers to cherish the play.
In the twilight's embrace, we find our true place,
Flight over horizons, a magical space.

So let the winds carry our spirits afar,
Through the painted horizon, we reach for the star.
In the canvas of time, we'll forever belong,
As we sing to the world our unyielding song.

A Symphony of Ethereal Tones

In the quiet hush of the evening's grace,
A symphony whispers through time and space.
Melodies linger in soft twilight,
Echoing magic, igniting the night.

Notes of the forest, a gentle refrain,
Carried on breezes, like falling rain.
Each rustling leaf plays a part in the score,
Inviting the heart to explore and restore.

Harmony dances in shadows and light,
Crafting a tapestry, vivid and bright.
With every heartbeat, the music unfolds,
Revealing the stories that nature holds.

Celestial bodies join in the song,
Creating a richness where dreams belong.
In the symphony's breeze, our spirits align,
With ethereal tones that forever entwine.

So close your eyes, let the music embrace,
In the whispers of night, find your own place.
For in every note lies a tale to be spun,
A symphony waiting, with each setting sun.

Whispers of Light Beneath Scaled Majesty

In shadows of mountains, whispers play,
The dragons above in their grand ballet.
With scales that shimmer like stars on high,
They dance through the night, painting the sky.

Echoes of magic weave through the air,
Soft murmurs of secrets, a tale to share.
Each flicker of flame, a story unfurled,
A glimpse of their power, a hint of their world.

Beneath the moonlight, they soar and glide,
Guardians of dreams, on wings they ride.
A promise of wonder in every flight,
As hearts stir with hope, igniting the night.

The earth holds its breath, as they roam free,
Nature's own magic, in harmony.
From valleys to peaks, their shadows entwine,
A dance of the ages, both fierce and divine.

So listen, dear wanderer, hear the call,
Of dragons above, watch, as they enthrall.
In whispers of light, beneath scaled majesty,
Lies the magic of worlds yet to be.

Mirage of Colors in a Celestial Ascent

Above the horizon, hues intertwine,
A symphony woven with threads divine.
The sun climbs slowly, igniting the day,
In a mirage of colors that softly sway.

Crimson and gold paint the heavens bright,
As daybreak unfolds its breathtaking sight.
The clouds, like brushstrokes, drift and twirl,
In a dance of perfection, as dreams unfurl.

Each moment a canvas, ever so rare,
Where the light meets the dark in a mystical flare.
A kaleidoscope whispers, a tune unconfined,
In this tapestry spun with the threads of the mind.

As the sky shifts and shimmers in glee,
A celestial ascent for all eyes to see.
The magic is fleeting, yet timeless in grace,
As colors collide in a vibrant embrace.

So let your heart soar on wings of delight,
In the mirage of colors, set your soul alight.
For hidden amongst every shimmering hue,
Are the dreams of the dawn, forever anew.

Ethereal Glow of Forgotten Legends

In whispers of ages, the legends reside,
With hearts full of stories, they patiently bide.
An ethereal glow in the shadows they find,
A tapestry woven of walkings entwined.

Beneath the starlit sky, the echoes resound,
Of heroes and trials, in whispers profound.
Their tales linger softly, like mist in the air,
An invitation to wander, to dream and to dare.

Through silent forests, where moonbeams stride,
The essence of glories walks side by side.
With branches that cradle the past in their keep,
In legends that shimmer, awake from deep sleep.

From valleys in shadows to mountains aglow,
The heart of the stories is all we must know.
So hold fast to the dreams, let them kindle the fire,
In the glow of the legends, our souls will aspire.

For lost in the whispers, their magic aligns,
With the breath of the ancients, in silvered designs.
In the ethereal glow, let your spirit ascend,
For forgotten legends are never the end.

Harmony of Light and Flight in Otherworldly Skies

Beneath a vast canvas of shimmering light,
Creatures take wing, in majestic flight.
With feathers that glisten in colors untold,
They weave through the heavens, both daring and bold.

A harmony flourishes, as day meets the night,
In whispers of breezes, they dance with delight.
In currents of wonder, they soar like a dream,
Where magic ignites in each silvery beam.

Through galaxies spun with threads of pure grace,
The freedom of flight in this infinite space.
With echoes of laughter that carry afar,
They spark with the brilliance of each shining star.

So glance at the heavens, where dreams intertwine,
In the flight of the souls, where the heart learns to shine.
Each moment a treasure that beckons to rise,
In the harmony of light within otherworldly skies.

With wings wide and open, let your spirit fly,
In the cradle of wonders, dance in the sky.
For life is a symphony, a gift that is free,
In the harmony of flight, find your melody.

Wings of Light

In the meadow where shadows play,
A whispering breeze leads the way.
Golden beams dance on the ground,
Dreams in the air softly found.

Beneath the arch of the azure sky,
Hope takes flight, learning to fly.
With every flutter, hearts will soar,
Chasing the sunlight, craving more.

Each petal blooms with colors bright,
A canvas painted in pure delight.
Where laughter lingers, joy ignites,
The world unfolds in wings of light.

Through the trees, a melody calls,
Echoing deep as twilight falls.
Magic stirs in each gentle breeze,
Awakening dreams with effortless ease.

With every dawn, fresh stories arise,
A tapestry woven beneath the skies.
In this realm of wonder, we find,
The gentle touch of a guiding mind.

Wings of Shade

In the quiet of the dusky hour,
Nature cloaked in tranquil power.
Whispers hidden beneath the leaves,
Secrets spun in twilight weaves.

Silent shadows dance and sway,
As the light begins to fray.
Every branch a story holds,
Mysteries wrapped in twilight folds.

With every rustle, a tale begins,
Of ancient dreams and wistful sins.
The nightingale sings a haunting song,
Echoing where the shadows long.

Beneath the boughs, all hearts entwine,
Finding romance in the dark divine.
A world reborn through muted grace,
In shadows deep, we find our place.

When the stars emerge, they softly glow,
Embracing the secrets we long to know.
In the arms of night, we quietly wait,
For the wings of shade to narrate our fate.

Mysteries in Every Shade

In the depths of a moonlit glen,
Where shadows gather, whispers blend.
Lost among the ferns and trees,
Lay secrets hidden on the breeze.

Chasing twilight's fading light,
Mysteries swirl in the soft twilight.
Each corner turned, a tale to find,
A thread that weaves through heart and mind.

Among the thickets, stories lie,
Of ancient times and places high.
The winds will carry forgotten lore,
In every shade, new realms to explore.

With a flicker of stars above,
The night ignites our dreams of love.
Each shadow holds a spark of truth,
A longing bound in eternal youth.

In the stillness, every heart feels,
The pulse of magic, perceptive wheels.
For in the dark, our spirits wade,
In life's embrace, the mysteries laid.

The Fables of the Cosmic Skylight

Beneath the vast and twinkling dome,
The universe sings of tales to roam.
Stars like lanterns burst in flight,
Whispering fables of the night.

Galaxies spin in a cosmic dance,
Every twinkle a forgotten chance.
In the silence, stories entwine,
Of heart and hope, of fate divine.

Meteors streak with a fleeting grace,
Chasing dreams through the darkest space.
Each wish cast on a shimmering beam,
Weaving the fabric of a celestial dream.

In every shadow, there's light to trace,
The harmony of time and place.
With every tale the universe shares,
We find our hearts in its vibrant snares.

Underneath this cosmic shroud,
We gather strength, proud and loud.
For in the depth of the endless night,
Are fables spun in the cosmic light.

Majestic Brushes of the Mystic

With strokes of wonder, the world unfolds,
A canvas alive with stories retold.
In twilight's glow, colors blend,
As fate and fortune dance and bend.

Nature sweeps on like an artist's hand,
Painting dreams on a shifting land.
In every hue, emotions dwell,
Where joy and sorrow meet, they swell.

Majestic shades in the morning dew,
Whisper secrets that feel so true.
Through sunflower fields, the breezes play,
Spinning webs where shadows sway.

With every dawn, the palette shifts,
Crafting wonders, giving gifts.
A brush dipped in the hues of fate,
Creating magic we contemplate.

In this world of colors bold,
Every moment, a story told.
With majestic brushes, the mystic creates,
A masterpiece that never abates.

Wings of Dappled Dreams

In twilight's hush, where shadows play,
Soft whispers dance on light's ballet.
A fleeting glimpse of what might be,
On feathered wings, we long to see.

The moonlit path calls out our name,
With every heartbeat, stokes the flame.
In dappled hues, our spirits soar,
To realms unknown, forevermore.

The gentle breeze, a lullaby,
That sweeps us up, to kiss the sky.
With dreams as bright as starlit streams,
We find our peace in dappled dreams.

Through sprawling fields and whispered sighs,
Where time is lost, and magic flies.
The stories blur like ink in rain,
And linger sweet within the grain.

Oh, take my hand, let's drift away,
To chase the dawn at break of day.
With every beat, our fates entwined,
In which our hopes and dreams aligned.

Celestial Shadows on Feathered Flight

A twilight haze wraps around the night,
Suspended dreams take graceful flight.
In shadows cast by moons so bright,
We chase the stars with pure delight.

Beneath the vast, embracing sky,
Our souls ascend, they flit and fly.
On feathered wings, we pierce the dark,
Igniting dreams, we leave a mark.

The ethereal glow of stardust trails,
Tells stories deep in whispered tales.
Through cosmic seas, we dare to glide,
With every wish, the worlds collide.

Among the clouds of silver sheen,
We find the places yet unseen.
Through cosmic dance and starry plight,
We weave our hopes on feathered flight.

Let time suspend as we partake,
In celestial realms, our dreams awake.
A journey stitched with threads of night,
Forever bound in the ethereal light.

Hues of the Mystic Sky

Beneath a canvas brushed with dreams,
Where every color surely gleams.
In shades of blue and violet's kiss,
We find the world wrapped in pure bliss.

The mountains sing in hues of gold,
As twilight whispers stories bold.
The stars emerge with gentle grace,
Each twinkling light, a warm embrace.

In painted skies where silence reigns,
Our hearts connect with whispered gains.
Through every hue, we seek to find,
The colors that unite mankind.

With every sunset, dreams ignite,
In mystic shades, we take delight.
Bright yellows and fiery reds,
In heavens wide, our spirits tread.

Let's paint our hopes in skyward swirls,
Where magic dances, and laughter twirls.
In hues of twilight, we take flight,
Embracing joy 'neath fading light.

Ethereal Striations Beneath Starlit Tides

Beneath the waves, a shimmer glows,
Where moonlight dances on watery prose.
In every ripple, secrets hide,
Ethereal striations, a mystic guide.

The sea unfolds its whispered dreams,
In gentle tides, the starlight beams.
Each wave a tale of ages past,
In ebb and flow, moments cast.

In tranquil depths where silence dwells,
The ocean sings its ancient spells.
With every surge, the stories glide,
Through cosmic dance on starlit tide.

Where colors blend and spirits blend,
The universe begins to mend.
In watery depths of dark and light,
Ethereal striations take their flight.

Let's weave our dreams with ocean's might,
And sail the currents to endless night.
In every wave, our hearts will glide,
And find our peace in starlit tide.

Whimsical Strokes in a Gaslight Glow

In the lantern's warm embrace,
Shadows flicker, softly trace.
Laughter dances in the air,
Magic lingers everywhere.

Spider silk of silvery thread,
Whispers of the dreams we've bred.
Each stroke glimmers, paints the night,
In gaslight's glow, all feels right.

Figures twist in twilight's hue,
Echoes of the things we knew.
Beneath the stars, a world unfurls,
Charming tales of boys and girls.

Gales of laughter, secrets shared,
Each heart laid bare, no one cared.
In this realm of whispered bliss,
Every moment, stolen kiss.

An artist's hand creates the dreams,
All is not as it seems.
With whimsical strokes, we explore,
In this gaslight, we seek more.

The Ornate Dance of Shadowed Light

Underneath a crescent moon,
Night unfolds, a gentle tune.
Figures clad in robes of night,
Join the dance of shadowed light.

Glistening stars begin to twinkle,
Phantom shapes begin to crinkle.
With each step, the world transforms,
As silence wraps in gentle norms.

Veils of mist embrace the ground,
Secrets whisper all around.
Every shadow, every glow,
Tells a story we don't know.

Time rewinds with every beat,
Softly binding heart and feet.
In this dance of dark and bright,
Life becomes a sheer delight.

With every twirl, a promise made,
Fancy dreams don't quickly fade.
In ornate grace, the spirits rise,
Beneath the gaze of endless skies.

Spectrum of the Ancient Beasts

Elusive shapes in rainbow shades,
From forest deep, their spirit fades.
Ancient whispers fill the air,
Tales of beasts beyond compare.

With eyes like jewels, bright and vast,
They traverse a world so fast.
In the night, their howls resound,
Echoes of the magic found.

From dragon's fire to gryphon's flight,
Mysteries embrace the night.
Colors swirl in wild ballet,
Spectrum dances, night and day.

Legends carved in twilight stone,
In every corner, histories grown.
Still they roam in dreams we weave,
In each tale, we dare believe.

The ancient call, a beckoning song,
Invites the brave, the true, the strong.
In their gaze, life intertwines,
Spectrum's dance in history's lines.

Flight of the Multicolored Spirits

Through the skies on wings of flame,
Spirits soar, wild and untame.
Dancing high on breezy trails,
Tales of hope within their sails.

Fluttering past the silver stars,
They weave the night with vibrant bars.
Colors blend in the moon's embrace,
Each heartbeat quickens, finds its place.

In the whispers of the night,
They carry dreams just out of sight.
With every flap, a wish takes flight,
Painting the dark with sheer delight.

In multicolored arcs, they play,
Filling gaps in night and day.
Bringing light to shadows born,
Life anew with every dawn.

So let them carry all your cheer,
These spirits vibrant, ever near.
In their flight, you'll find your heart,
A tapestry of dreams to start.

Palette of the Hidden Horizon

In twilight's grasp the colors blend,
A world unspoken, where dreams transcend.
Beyond the hills, where shadows play,
A whispered secret calls the day.

The canvas waits with bated breath,
As stars awaken from their rest.
With every stroke, a tale unfurls,
Of hidden lands and magic swirls.

Beneath the sky of azure deep,
The threads of fate and courage creep.
In every hue, a hope ignites,
To sail beyond the starry nights.

Through forests dense and rivers wide,
The palette pulses, a hidden guide.
With every color, life reborn,
In harmony, the world adorn.

So venture forth, embrace the glow,
For in the dark, the colors flow.
A journey waits, with wonders sown,
In palette dreams, we find our own.

Hushed Colors in the Dragon's Dance

In silence deep, the dragons glide,
With wings like whispers, they turn the tide.
Their scales aglow with hues unseen,
In twilight's hold, they reign supreme.

Against the dusk, their shadows weave,
A tapestry of magic, we believe.
With every beat of dragon's heart,
The colors shift, and dreams depart.

Emerald green and sapphire blue,
In the dragon's dance, old tales renew.
A flicker of gold, a flash of red,
Through quiet skies, their legends spread.

In swirling mist, the night takes flight,
With hushed colors, they steal the light.
Each graceful move, a stroke of grace,
In harmony, they find their space.

As dawn breaks forth, the colors fade,
But in our hearts, their dance is laid.
A memory etched in every glance,
A fleeting dream, the dragon's dance.

Shimmering Hues of Mythic Realms

In ancient woods where legends grow,
The shimmering hues begin to flow.
With every leaf that flutters down,
A story whispered, a hero's crown.

Across the skies of twilight's glow,
The colors pulse and ebb, then flow.
In realms where myth and dreams collide,
A tapestry of magic's tide.

A phoenix bright, aflame with light,
In golden hues, it takes to flight.
With every rise, a realm reborn,
In shimmering hues, a new dawn sworn.

Beneath the stars, the shadows dance,
In mythic realms, they seek their chance.
A symphony of color sings,
Of ancient lore and hidden wings.

So close your eyes and drift away,
To where the shimmering colors play.
In every hue, a wish takes form,
In mythic realms, our dreams are warm.

Fantasia of the Feathered Titan

In skies aloft, a titan flies,
With feathers bright that paint the skies.
A fantasia of wings unfurled,
In vibrant colors, dreams are swirled.

With every flap, the heavens sigh,
A melody that bids goodbye.
In sunset's glow, the titan soars,
Through whispered tales of distant shores.

With hues of amber, crimson flare,
The feathered giant leaves its care.
In glorious arcs, it writes the lore,
Of ancient hearts and battles' roar.

Among the clouds, the titan dwells,
In harmony where magic swells.
With every beat, a new path calls,
In this fantasia, wonder sprawls.

So lift your gaze, let spirits rise,
To where the titan greets the skies.
In colors bold, let dreams ignite,
In feathered flight, embrace the light.

Shadowed Drifts of Chromatic Tales

In shadows deep where colors fade,
The whispers of old stories laid.
Through twilight's grasp and twilight's light,
The hues of dreams take daring flight.

A river flows with colors bold,
Each ripple speaks of truths untold.
With every shade a secret keeps,
Of ancient lands where silence sleeps.

In every corner, magic stirs,
With laughter soft and softest purrs.
A tapestry of dusk and dawn,
Where every thread a legend's drawn.

The moonlight dances on the streams,
Reflecting all our secret dreams.
With every twist and wisp of air,
The past and present blend with care.

So venture forth where colors blend,
Embrace the tales that time may send.
For in this realm where shadows twine,
Your heart will find what's truly thine.

The Breath of Colorful Beasts

In fields where mythical ones roam,
Each beast a tale, each breath a home.
Their vibrant coats in sunlit beams,
Reveal the magic of our dreams.

With wings of fire and eyes of gold,
They carry stories yet untold.
A lion roars, to skies so vast,
Unraveling the threads of past.

The phoenix rises, blaze anew,
In every feather, every hue.
Their whispers call from land to sea,
A tapestry of what could be.

Through glens of green the creatures dart,
With gentle grace, they steal the heart.
A fleeting glimpse, a fleeting glance,
In every moment, magic's dance.

So let your spirit wander wide,
To find the beasts, the colors guide.
In dreams they blossom, vibrant, free,
A world of wonder waits for thee.

Dusk's Prism in Flight

At dusk when day begins to wane,
The sky ignites with soft refrain.
A prism forms, a dance of light,
Where day and night take sweet delight.

The clouds, like whispered secrets, glide,
On currents where the shadows bide.
With every hue, a story told,
Of brave journeys and hearts of gold.

The stars arise with timid grace,
Painting the twilight's gentle face.
They sprinkle dreams like dust so fine,
Transforming darkness into shine.

A soft wind stirs, begins to sigh,
As twilight dances in the sky.
With colors swirling, hearts will soar,
In dusk's embrace, we yearn for more.

So linger here in twilight's glow,
Where secrets of the evening flow.
In whispers soft and gentle flight,
We find our peace in dusky light.

Fantasia of Ethereal Resonance

In dreams where echoes softly play,
A melody of night and day.
With notes that shimmer, spark, and twine,
We weave the past, both yours and mine.

The stars compose their mystic song,
In realms where we all long to belong.
With every beat, the heart aligns,
To rhythms lost in ancient signs.

Through air so sweet, the whispers weave,
Of tales that none could dare believe.
In every sigh, a chance to find,
The beauty held within the mind.

When night descends, the magic glows,
In vibrant hues that life bestows.
A dance of dreams, ethereal nights,
Where every spark ignites delights.

So close your eyes and drift away,
To lands where wonders brightly play.
In resonance, our spirits sing,
In this fantastical offering.

Radiant Veils in the Evening Breeze

In twilight's glow, a shimmer weaves,
Soft whispers dance among the leaves.
Each petal held, a tale untold,
Beneath the sky's embrace of gold.

The stars emerge with silent grace,
While shadows play their spectral chase.
A gentle breeze caresses night,
As dreams take wing on soft starlight.

The moon above, a watchful eye,
Guides wayward hearts as they pass by.
In silver beams, the world transforms,
As magic stirs, the heart now warms.

Veils of wonder wrap the earth,
In each breath, a spark of mirth.
Radiance blooms where hopes ignite,
In evening's dance, all feels just right.

So linger near, let spirits soar,
In radiant hues, we'll venture more.
For in this realm where dreams take flight,
We find our place in endless night.

Twilight's Tapestry of Flapping Secrets

In twilight's hush, the secrets fly,
On whispered wings through dusk-lit sky.
The shadows shift, they twist and twine,
A spectral dance, both sweet and fine.

Threads of stories, woven tight,
Underneath the cloak of night.
Each fluttered flap, a spell, a clue,
As twilight wraps the old in new.

The breeze carries a feathered sound,
Echoes lost and whispers found.
Hidden realms within the dark,
Where nightingale sings and dreams embark.

A tapestry of stars unfurls,
As wonders brush the sleeping swirls.
With every glance, the world transforms,
Embracing mysteries in quiet forms.

So pause and listen, heed the call,
For secrets linger, great and small.
In twilight's cloak, we find the key,
To realms of magic, wild and free.

Luminescent Drifts Across the Void

In vast expanse where starlight flows,
Luminescent drifts, the cosmos glows.
Each spark ignites a tale anew,
Across the void, where dreams breakthrough.

With whispers echoing through the night,
Galaxies swirl in a dance of light.
Mysteries wrapped in twilight's gaze,
Casting spells in the moon's soft haze.

Comets trail like tears of joy,
Embracing night, their hearts deploy.
Through velvet skies, they weave and roam,
As cosmic wanderers seek their home.

Floating softly, the shadows play,
In luminescent hues, they sway.
Each drift a moment in endless time,
A cosmic journey, a silent rhyme.

So gaze aloft with wonder's sight,
As luminescent dreams alight.
In the expanse, we find our part,
An everlasting dance, a beating heart.

Kaleidoscopic Traces in the Midnight Air

In midnight's grasp, the colors bloom,
Kaleidoscopic traces lighten gloom.
With every turn, the patterns shift,
As spirits twirl in a radiant lift.

Whirls of dreams sprout in the night,
Cascading hues in playful flight.
Each vivid stroke, a story shared,
In the canvas sky, our hopes are bared.

The air is rich with shimmering tones,
As shadowed paths reveal their homes.
With every breath, the magic drapes,
Around our hearts, the wonder shapes.

So dance with me, let colors swirl,
In midnight air, let laughter twirl.
Embrace the night, where dreams take form,
In kaleidoscopic hues, we're warm.

Each fleeting glimpse, a vivid thread,
In the fabric of the night we tread.
Through vibrant strokes, our wishes sweep,
In midnight's air, our hearts we keep.

The Harmonious Glide of Enigma

In twilight's grasp, shadows dance,
Whispers of dreams, a fleeting chance.
Secrets entwined in the gentle breeze,
Silent echoes, the mind's tease.

Through tangled woods where wonders dwell,
Mysteries twist like an ancient spell.
A glimmering path where few have trod,
Leading to realms where hopes are awed.

Stars flicker tales beyond the night,
Each glint a promise, a hidden light.
Underneath the canvas, worlds collide,
In the harmonious glide of enigma wide.

The moon whispers soft, a lullaby sweet,
Wrapped in the dreams where shadows meet.
A journey awakes with dawn's embrace,
To find the magic, to trace the lace.

Gazing into the Celestial Canvas

Beyond the veil, up in the skies,
Constellations weave their ancient ties.
Galaxies swirl in a cosmic dance,
Each twinkle a story, a lifelong chance.

The tapestry glimmers, a vibrant hue,
Wonders entangled, ever anew.
Whispers of stardust, soft and clear,
Call forth the dreamers, draw them near.

With every comet that streaks through night,
Hope takes flight in its radiant light.
Gazing up, hearts intertwined,
Finding the magic the heavens designed.

In nebula's cradle, where wishes glow,
The secrets of time in the starlight flow.
Drifting through realms where spirits convene,
Embracing the wonders, serene and unseen.

Tales of Colors Forgotten

Once in a world of vibrant hue,
A palette of dreams, where laughter grew.
Colors entwined, a joyous song,
Yet time weaves threads that don't belong.

Violet whispers in the twilight's sigh,
Once bright and bold, now fading nigh.
Echoes of laughter, colors untold,
In memory's chest, their stories unfold.

Crimson petals fall, a soft refrain,
From gardens of joy to fields of grain.
For every hue, a tale lies bare,
In the hush of dusk, and the morning air.

The winds carry stories through autumn's chill,
Of faded rainbows and dreams to fulfill.
Through shadowed alleys of heart and mind,
We seek the colors that time left behind.

Enchanted Drift of Chromatic Wings

In meadows rich with whispers light,
Butterflies flutter in day's delight.
Chromatic wings, they gleam and sway,
Painting the air in a bright ballet.

A journey begun on a sunbeam's glance,
Each flutter a step in the world's dance.
Nature's brush strokes the canvas wide,
With every beat, the heart takes pride.

Through valleys deep where laughter flows,
In every hue, the spirit grows.
Crimson, azure, gold, and green,
A tapestry woven in light unseen.

As twilight beckons, wings take flight,
In the dimming glow of approaching night.
The enchanted drift, a tale unfurled,
With chromatic dreams, they embrace the world.